WHOL  D

Who

By

Ian McCormack

Published by

KRATOS PUBLISHERS

WHOLE HEARTED

All bible scripture quotation are from authorized King James Version and unless otherwise indicated are taken from the English Standard Version.

Published By

KRATOS PUBLISHERS

CONTENT PAGE

INTRODUCTION

The glory of God gives off light, Moses saw that glory and he was transformed, but I had the amazing opportunity to understand the waves of light that came off the glory; the first wave of light that came into me was absolute **comfort**. The comfort came so deeply into me that all the sense of false comfort was literally washed away. The next wave that came into me was complete **peace**; absolute, total, unadulterated peace from the top of my head to the base of my feet. As I moved into the light closer to the Lord, I felt **Joy** and when I came into His presence and saw the glory of God and the fullness of the glory, I then found **unconditional love**, absolute pure love. That love began to flow into me, when I realized how much I didn't love myself, I didn't believe I was worthy enough to be in His presence and as I continued to speak out from my heart, the love became stronger and in that love was an acceptance, an incredible acceptance that he loved me.

I began telling God all my failings, all my sin and the mess I made, His love didn't stop and what I found, I found Him filling my vessel up. Literally what I found was almost like a tide mark, I can feel the love somehow filling my spiritual being from my feet, up to my ankles, up to my knees, to my belly, my chest and I then began to weep uncontrollably. I then found that love was so powerful that it had filled me up till overflowing. I then had the amazing sense of well-being to open my eyes, as I opened my eyes; I saw that the light had not only filled me but was literally spilling out of me and was surrounding me 2 to 3 feet around me. Now, we had to be transformed from glory to glory and we love because He first loved us.

WITHIN THE VEIL

I then stepped into the cloud of Glory which would be termed in the New Testament and the Old "within the veil" and there was a veil of light which had like miniature stars, and when those miniature stars touched me and moved into me, I felt my broken heart being healed. I looked for love in many different places. How many know, if you love someone you give your heart to them? So here my heart was actually being healed in my heart of hearts. As I came through this veil of intense radiance which caused my own spiritual being to be eclipsed. I then saw in the centre of that the Lord, in His presence, purity, absolute purity. We should be pure because He is pure. Now I tried to be pure under my own strength, of my own good works, absolute failure. As I moved closer towards the Lord, what was coming out of His face, because it says that his face is literally like the sunshine in his full strength that the glory of the Father; is revealed in the face of Christ, the Holy Spirit glorifies the Son, the actual Son glorifies the Father.

And what was coming out was **holiness,** incredible holiness. To a person who had failed morally, holiness and purity were very abstract words, but to experience holiness, I was transformed. We should be holy because He is holy, how can we possibly be holy? By seeing him. Remember when Moses steps in the burning bush, He said "You are standing on what?"

Holy ground. How did the ground become holy? He the Lord God Almighty is holy. You come into his presence you all will be made holy. Christ in us, to make us holy. John said "I didn't see a temple, I saw the LORD".

> **Rev 21:22** And I saw no temple therein: for the Lord God Almighty and the Lamb are the temple of it.
> (KJV)

Then he stepped aside and began to open the new heavens and the new earth, I was then back in my body and I was absolutely transformed.

KINGDOM OF HEAVEN ON EARTH

I was then taken to church by a friend and I stood at the back of the church, I came up to the very front and the radiance of heaven came down. The light filled me, as I opened my eyes whilst on earth. The kingdom of heaven was within me, around me and filling me up at the same time. The love was coming to me as the Christians began praying for me. It just filled me, I then began to realize that I could have His presence.

As I then continued with the call of God and to minister, I came to the point where I felt very quickly in my Christian life, as though I was being sucked dry.

So, the simplicity of my first love and marriage to the Lord, the honeymoon period has suddenly changed. People were actually looking to me to meet their needs. They want you to pray for them, they want you to minister to them and they want you to prophesy and see their life and tell them what you are hearing from God for them. I was quite enjoying that moment. Seeing people get heal, I was getting more excited by the whole deal, but the trouble is as you get more and more known, how many know more and more people want to hear.

DIVIDED HEART

So what struck me was, I'll go to a meeting and somehow get the lines and lines and lines and lines and I'm praying and prophesying, the power of God falling and I was shocked, I thought I'll finish that line and I will turn around there's another line, then I realize that half the congregation was sitting out there waiting for me to actually finish praying for them and then they will get up. Sometimes I prayed for 3 to 4 hours, I was thinking God this is a fascinating scenario and then I continued on and then got married and I began to think I feel as though there's so many demands upon my vessel, I feel like am being sucked dry from the church, from the relationship, from the body of Christ people needing etc.

I came to the point that; God I'm not even sure about this whole thing, what's going on? He said, "You have a divided heart, He said that your heart is divided." I said NO, I am wholehearted, I am on fire, I mean. You got the wrong man; I am a zealot. Once again, He said you have a divided heart, and I say okay show me my heart; (big mistake!) Suddenly I saw a earthenware vessel and in that vessel, I saw cocked taps, five of them, ever seen these wine caskets were they have tap the wine comes in?

I'm looking at this vessel and I said God what's that? He said that's your heart. I watched wine or presence coming into that vessel, I watched it coming down and pouring out of that earthenware vessel through those taps and they're on full. As I look at that vessel a little bit closer, I can see it was also dripping wine through cracks that had appeared in the base of the vessel. I said God what on earth is this about? He said that's your life, He said my presence is coming into you and you are like a funnel, my presence is flowing straight through you into people and things you have given your heart to.

MARRIAGE

You have a divided heart, I said well then, what on earth is that tap representing? He said, "That's your wife, He said the world tells you, if you love someone, you give them your heart. So, when you got married you gave your heart to your wife. He said but you learn not to put all your eggs in one basket. You have given part of your heart to your wife, He said, how has it been so far in the first six months of marriage? I thought "well" time out. I said it was quite interesting, It was a lot easier being single, you know what I mean, I said there seems to be a mystery here called marriage. I haven't quite figured this one out and I said, but I prayed in the Lord, the Lord gave me out of John 17 and I think it was that the two shall become one. You know what I mean? as he was with the father, his prayer for us is that we will be one. I said well, we're trying to become one here, but it seems like we're kind of missing each other. He said well, have you hurt her? I said well, it seems like it. He said; has she hurt you? I said well most likely more than anyone else so far on the planet. How many of you know those close to you are the ones that can do the most damage? Cause you drop your guards. So, I said okay. I understand that a little, she is pretty tentative, six months and the honeymoon period is over. He said well, I gave you a picture of two earthenware vessels been dropped in the furnace didn't I? Before you got married? I said, yes, you did. He said what happened to you when you were looking at the vision? I said well I got so tired looking at the vision because all I saw was the earthenware vessels gone and the flames coming up out of this kiln.

He said when you were about to look away, what did you see appear? I said, I saw one big golden vessel. He said it was quite a period before it became one golden vessel. It doesn't happen overnight.

FAMILY LOVE

Okay God what's the second one? He said that's your mother. He said, well you love your mother, your mother prayed you into the kingdom, you honour her as a woman of God, you honour her because she loves you and you, although you have left your mother and married your wife. Part of your heart, is still in your mother. I said that's interesting, that's exactly true. He said your wife has got two for the price of one, she got you and your mother. So, I feel like I've got two for the price of one, I got her and her mother. He said, who has your heart and who have you given your heart to? I said, whoa! I said that's true, my mother has part of my heart.

CHURCH OBLIGATIONS

I said "What's this?" He said that's the church. He said, you love the church? You didn't before of course, but when you got saved, you saw the body of Christ following Jesus, the bride of Christ. You love the church and you want to serve the church to see the return of Christ, you lay your life down for it. And I said, that's true. He said; how has it been so far? I said quite interesting. He said well what's happened with a bunch of Christians? How have you experienced them? I said well, some of them haven't been the (most) sweetest people on the planet and He said, see the cracks on the vessels? And I said yes, He said how many of them come up to you and demanded you pray for them and when you say, look I'm exhausted and I got nothing, they have smashed into you? I said, that's true. He said do you feel damaged by Christians demanding? I said, well, yes. He said that as a lifeguard, what were lifeguards taught when a drowning person came up to them? I said, we were taught to basically knock him out and put him in a full nelson. Because when you come up to a drowning person as a lifeguard, they think you're an island and try and climb up on top of you. Many lifeguards are drowned saving drowning people, because they are so desperate. They desperately have their needs and sight completely and absolutely focused on themselves. The desperation they are dying and so anyone who comes up to save them, they can kill the person saving them.

EVANGELISM

What's this? And this is the fourth tap. He said, that is the lost. You got saved out of the world you realized that everyone in the world doesn't know the Lord, bunch of Christians having holy huddles. Your desire is to get out there and save as many souls as possible, cause they are in darkness, you want to bring them back in and I said, that's true.

EXTRA CURRICULAR ACTIVITY

Let's see, what's this one? He said; sport; fishing, you diving, you're hunting, you're surfing, you're sailing. He said, what does your heart look like right now? I said, I think it's divided. He said, how much of your heart do you think you've given me? if you took out your wife, your mother, the church, the lost and sport, I said 10%.

PERCENTAGE OF LOVE

He said, what's the greatest commandment? And I said, well the Bible says: "The greatest commandment is to love the Lord thy God with all thy heart, with all thy mind, with all thy strength, then to love our neighbours, as ourselves". He said if you've only given 90%, how much is all? I said 100%. He said, you're only giving me 10% and you give 90% to them. How on earth if I take my heart back from my wife, my mother, the church, the loss, sports. How the heck can I love them? Sure, if you love someone you give them your heart. He said: well the greatest commandment to love me with all your heart. How many hearts have you got son? I said, I got one. I said you mean if I take it back and give it to you, what will happen? He said let me show you, He said where your treasure is, there your heart is.

He said if you put your heart that has been before you were a Christian into sex, drugs and rock and roll and surf. Now you've replaced it with what appears to be Godly things and good things, family, friends, body of Christ.

He said what happens if you give it to me? I said well, you'll most likely heal, because you heal the broken-hearted. So, where your treasure is there your heart is. He said if you give your heart to me, what will I give back? I thought **love.** He said you love because I first loved you. Suddenly the penny dropped, I said to God, if I give my whole heart to you and take it back, what will my vessel look like? Instantly I saw a new vessel; no taps, no cracks. I saw a whole vessel and I watched this incredible presence flying out of Heaven down into the vessel and I watched it beginning to fill up. As I began to watch it filling up, I could remember distinctly standing in heaven and feeling that experience of being filled up. He said give unto God and I'll give unto you pressed down, shaken together and running over. I thought they only do that in church when they want money. I've never heard it talked about the heart. He said I'm not interested in your money, he said I'm interested in you. You give your entire life to me, you give your heart to me son and I'll give it to you a hundred-fold, pressed down, shaken together and running over.

NO MORE PERFORMANCE, CONTROL OR MANIPULATION

He said most of you live as a funnel. He said I want you to have not a trickle coming out of you. I want rivers of living water. Then He said; the key to that is to guard your heart, but who are you supposed to give your heart to? The Lord, how many knows it's very hard for anyone to get hurt if you give your heart to God? Do you know you are not trying to please or perform or strive for someone else's attention or love, when you are actually getting it from him? How many of you know it takes out the whole performance orientated acceptance and that you're living off other people? How many of you know;

"Christ is sufficient for me"? Your identity, your self-worth, your entire well-being and confidence is actually in Him. We often try and find our identity in people and our acceptance and we try and top up our love from human beings. Our love tanks goes down to empty. Who do we look to, to fill our love tank up? God is love.

People want touch, feeling, hands on love. I said, well, that's a bonus. Because that's often manipulative, fickle and conditional. But God's love is unconditional. He said when you stood before me son, what did I give you? I said "unconditional love". He said, can you improve on that love? Is there anything you can do in the church and preaching and ministry and praying, prophesying? Can you improve the love I had for you when you died a complete sinner saved by grace and stood at my presence? I said big fat ZERO.

TRUST IN MAN VS TRUST IN GOD

He said; that will take striving out of you because you enter the rest of the Lord, I can do nothing apart from him. And if you rest in him through obedience and love relationship things will change. So anyhow, I'm staying here with all this download, Lord said give me your heart. I said, why? He said take your heart back from your wife, your mother, the church, the loss. I said praise God, I am free.

But then as I was doing it, I said isn't it selfish, it's all for me. He said you can do nothing apart from me.

We love because he first loved us. So I stood up, prayed this prayer, gave my heart back to the Lord and instantly I was back in the realm of glory and the presence of God. I was free from any form of expectation, performance, control, domination, manipulation; free.

So, I then turned to my wife and said I'm free. She looked at me; she said "I feel like you've pulled your heart away from me. I said I have; I gave it to God. Have you got a problem?

Reason why is because we are looking to man to meet the desperate need for affection and love and acceptance. Cursed is the man who trusts in man, blessed is the man who trusts in the Lord.

My dear wife suddenly got the revelation short time after and realize she'd given her heart to me and to mum and the Christian people she had been with in the church all her life and she suddenly realized, how she looked to Christians and spiritual moms and her own mum before she looked to God. Why? Because whoever got your heart is who you going to look too. And I began to realize that people had given their hearts to children. When those children left and got married. He better look after my dear darling child! Or I'll kill him. I then saw people that put their hearts into animals; touch my pet, or the pet would die and then devastation happens to them, then I saw old people;

one would die the other one dies shortly after, what's all this about? Who's got your heart? This was 21 years ago, and I speak again to see the desperation of how this went down through grandchildren, great-grand. I mean we're talking an amazing amount of things that are affecting people's heart and what they'd put their heart into, to find acceptance and love, meaning and purpose.

I saw an incredible amount of striving in ministry, people competing, climbing on top of each other to get positions in the body of Christ because of the need to have a sense of acceptance. So actually, trying to perform for God.

SCRIPTURE REFERENCE ON HEART

God said it's all to do with the heart. He said begin reading it. He wants an understanding of a whole heart; create in me a clean heart, because the pure in heart shall see God. He loves a broken and contrite heart one that's humble before him. He says that you've treasured my word in your heart, the word of God was a treasure in the heart, and Jesus is the word of God. The treasure was in our heart, the treasure of great price. Watch over your heart with all diligence because out of it comes the wellspring of life.

A joyful heart, in fact, the heart is more deceitful than all. That's why you need to ask God, show me my heart because it's the Holy Spirit that searches out even the heart of God and he knows the heart of all men. Where your treasures are is where your heart is.

Mary pondered these things in her heart when these prophetic words came, she pondered them and she actually treasured all these things in her heart. It is with the heart you believe in the salvation that Christ may dwell in your heart, Christ in you, you in him. Where is the kingdom of God? It's not of this world, it's not of this realm; It's an interesting mystery in itself, isn't it? The kingdom of God is another realm but that kingdom of God has come unto you. You are a garden that God wants to be a spring in the well, He wants to walk with you in the secret place in your Garden of Eden in your heart. To meet with him in the secret place like song of songs, song of songs going in there and meeting with him in that place. My beloved is mine and I am his, you hear me? And I will run after him, I will search after him, seek after him as a lover. As a deep intimate lover, that he might know you, you might know him which is eternal life. you might actually pursue him as the deer pants for the water, so my soul longs after the Lord. The whole thing of marriage, I am to be preparing myself as a bride for a marriage with him to be married to the Lord, one with him.

PEOPLE, ANIMALS, HOUSES IN HEAVEN

There is no marriage in heaven, we are to be as Angels, one with Him.

People ask me; when you went to heaven did you see family members, did you see loved ones? I asked God why they asked me that? He said, because when they die, they're more interested in seeing their loved ones, because that's where their heart is. and they said well, do you know if my family member got to heaven? I thought well I don't know, God knows that. What if they went to hell? How could God do that? And I realize that a number of them could hate God because the person they loved and put their treasure into could potentially be in hell, so they couldn't possibly love a God that would send someone to hell. Then I began to watch a bunch of people praying to try and talk to the dead because what they're trying to do is connect with the people that they love. Some people came out to me and asked, did you see animals in heaven? Why do we want to see spot, rover and you know puss, you know what Skippy who knows what the heck is down there. And I said, God why will they ask me about animals? He said, it's because that's where their heart is. That's where the treasure is. Some said, did you see your house in heaven? what? I thought

I don't even like living in homes, I'm an outdoor person and I said, God why? And He said, because some put their treasures in the home. It's what they have lived for, work for and put their entire life and heart into building a house here on earth and they want to see how big it is up there. I said why on earth do you want a house. Anyhow, but I will say is that God neither slumbers nor sleeps, if there's no need to sleep? Why on earth do you want a house for? Ah! I just lost track of it all. Now the multitude of questions, I think God what on earth is going on with this talk why they asked me some of these? I've just seen Christ glorified, and they want to know about puss or the cat or the horse or something.

GOD SEES THE HEART

Where your treasure is, it's where your heart is. What on earth are you living for? Where are you? What are you praying for? Praying for a man, what to do? Love you so that you can give your heart to him. What are you looking for woman of God, a man of God? What are you thinking? I sought the Lord and I got a beautiful woman of God, the best out there, one in a million. You seek the face of God and He will add all these things unto you. What is your focus?

God looks at the heart, God knows the secrets of the heart, He even searches the motivation of the heart. And the intent of the heart but our heart is deceitfully wicked. So he wants to get to the motivation, the intent of your heart. If you've been controlled and dominated, you don't want anyone else to be in charge of you. Unless you forgive them and your heart gets healed, you will see anyone with strength and you won't want it, because you think: are they going to control me? So, you control your environment, so that you have the environment around you so controlled, that no one can possibly hurt you. You know what the basis of love is? **Trust**, if you can't trust God, you have a great difficulty in the area of love. God looks at the intent of the heart, one of the most bizarre things I got when I got saved and I couldn't understand it, was...when I got saved and got back into my body and I was in a house with two men and these men were talking in the kitchen, as I heard them talking I heard four conversations. I heard what they were saying out to each other but I could hear another conversation going on between these two men, about what they thought of each other and about what they actually thought about the whole deal here. I looked at them and said, but what on earth is that? He said, you are seeing people with a new heart and new light. You're actually seeing their heart, out of the abundance of the heart the mouth speaks. So when you died and went to heaven, how did the speech come? I said from my heart. They can hear what was going on in my heart in speech.

I mean you could actually hear the intent and motivation of the heart, how many people know that people put fronts and masquerades and faces up? So wonderful to see you today. Just oh my dear Lord, where did that knife come from? Knives in the eyes because out of the heart, there's the eyes are the windows of the soul. So the masquerade of the front of man is putting this whole bizarre façade up, and what are you doing? You're deceiving yourself and you're actually speaking a lie.

HOME OF THE HEART

The pure in heart shall see God, how will you like to see as God sees? How many of you would like revelation of the Heavens? How would you like to see the glory of God? The Lord changed my heart, the eyes of the heart. He wants to see revelation. The eyes of your heart may be enlightened and open to have revelation of the kingdom of God. You want to have the ears to hear what the spirit says, but the key to it is that, you have the heart of Christ. Take out the heart of stone, give me a heart of flesh, the eyes of the Lord looks across the earth looking for a heart who is wholly devoted to him. You want to do exploits for God, you want to lift your vision higher, you want to change the world, you want to actually bring revival. Guess what? Lord change my heart; Lord I give you my heart. He who loves the world, the love of the Father is not in him. The pride of life, the boastfulness, the riches of the world; the love of the Father is not in you. But we are sojourners, travellers. If your heart is in heaven, how many know you just passing through the planet?

Home is where? Heaven is my home. Then you going to deal with this in the Spirit, is not just words you can rattle off all the scriptures you like and meaningless meditation and repetition and proclamation, that means absolutely zero to the kingdom of Heaven into the spirit world, if you haven't aligned these words in your Spirit and they have become living words that you've eaten and it has become part of you, you have treasured and they have become your daily bread, and that word will cut.

OVERFLOWING

As I watched this vessel overflowing, I saw other vessels around it appear and I watched the Living Waters coming out of this vessel pouring into other vessels. I said: God what's that? It was like champagne glasses. He said, that's your mother, that's your father, that's your brother, that's your sister, that's your wife, that's your mother-in-law. Do you understand? a love that would not only meet the needs of those around you out of an overflow, but it could actually overflow to complete strangers and to the world. Does That helped a little bit, how can you continually give,

give, give? because it's actually coming out of an overflow. How many of you know when the overflow stops and you feel like you're an empty shell? Be real! I say to people, am not praying for you I got big fat zip. Let me step out of here for a few moments and get in touch with the presence of God, because if I can't, I'm wasting my time and your time even considering praying for you because basically, you only get a lovely nice one bunch of Christian platitudes and God bless you my son.

EYES ON JESUS

People turn from looking to you because you can have dependency and feel worthwhile because people need you. That might be your sense of importance of actual acceptance because they need you. You know what? They don't need you, they don't need me, they need God. You can point them pass the jellyfish man and pass something that they think they've seen and point them to Jesus, we might actually have some moves of God taking place. the heart of the man is turned towards the father Where can my help come from? From the Lord creator of Heaven and Earth.

Imagine a church of people on fire, seeking the face of God, being transparent, open and being willing to be real in their heart and actually connect with God and find their existence and their meaning and their love and acceptance directly in HIM. Not in what you do, not in your position, not in anything that you do but there's a complete rest that I will be happy to do absolutely nothing and still be completely content to be in Christ.

I'd be very happy to sit on a boat, fish every day and see no Christians or go anywhere near them. I'd be a happy camper, a pig in mud. I could man a lighthouse. But I can't, because it is no longer; I that live, Christ lives in me. To be absent from the body was better in many ways to be present with the Lord than to be here. Paul said that I'm here for who's benefit, not my own. No longer I that live, but Christ lives in me. Change my heart that I might love as you love, that I might see as you see, that I might minister as you minister, that I might be one with you and then I decrease that you might increase. Less of me; more of you, more love. But I tell you what, there's a place you have to discern the heart and whether you like it or not, the sword of the spirit comes against the intent and motivation of the heart and cuts between the soul and the Spirit.

IDENTITY IN GOD

So, He began to show us that as you work in your spirit, you can be free from manipulation and control coming down generational lines and through spiritual connections, soul ties with friends you've given your heart to. Through repentance and bringing your heart back, the Holy Spirit can come like a sword, the Word of God could cut and you can be free from that control. How many love to be free from control, manipulation, domination, all of the above? How many know that everyone else has got an agenda for your life? Would be nice to find God's agenda.

Our job as Christians is to find out what God has given to you, what God has spoken to you and as best we can help to facilitate that. The greatest leader is to be the greatest servant. Those who control and dominate are full of Saul, fear and demons. Those are more interested about their own self-importance and their own self-worth have actually lost sight of the fact that is the kingdom of God and is not your kingdom or your ministry that God is interested about, because God gives it and then he says kill it. He gives the promise and then says kill it. I've seen so many people fight all their life for their promise and their gifts and their calling and when it comes to killing it,

NO, that's from hell. The promise came, the Father killed it. Abraham heard the promise come, the father went to kill it. You better have it in your heart to have killed it because if you don't, it becomes your identity. And if someone takes that ministry off you, that's your baby and you'll kill. If anyone threatens your position or your name, you will kill for it.

So, Father we pray that you change our hearts, so we would have a heart that loves you. No other, that we will understand what love is all about? We actually begin to meet the person who can fulfil and heal and draw us into the glory of God, and Lord, I'm amazed in Ezekiel, It says: The glory of God came into the temple and as the glory of God came, a river came out.

RIVER OF LOVE

The River of Life, river of healing, a river of salvation, a river of blessing. Lord may our temple, our body, our vessel be ones that are literally able to hold and contain within it, the Glory of God because our heart is in YOUR hands, YOUR kingdom come, YOUR presence, YOU are glorified. When we have our hearts in YOUR hands and as healed by you and protected. Then you begin to then move through the motivation of the intent of the heart, then you give back to us pure love that's been cleansed and washed under the Blood of the Lamb and the love that comes out Lord doesn't have an agenda, a love that doesn't have an expectation, a love that doesn't control, a love that is not jealous or envious, a love that's not competitive, a love that does not in any way come against you and your purposes but seeks to see your love fill every other vessel around them, that they might be saved and healed and delivered, and that we might be the one who carries the overflowing presence of God in us, and those who look to you should be radiant and we pray Lord that the Shekinah Glory of God will fill us individually and then corporately that we might truly be ones that are light in this world and see the Light of

Christ shine that you might be glorified. That you might draw all men unto yourself, Christ in us the hope of glory. Teach us your mysteries Lord, teach us your way, show us the most important thing. Its our heart, our heart is wholly devoted to you and that you will look upon us and move through us with your glory and power because Christ in us, nothing is impossible in Jesus precious name, Amen.